PRAY TELL

Poems • Travis McCullers

Library of Congress Control Number: 2014959953

ISBN: 978-0-9857703-6-5

Pray Tell, by Travis McCullers

Published by Summerfield Publishing, New Plains Press

PO Box 1946

Auburn, AL 36831-1946

Newplainspress.com

for
Frank C. Davis Jr.

With gratitude
Johnny Summerfield, Nancy McCullers, and Frank C. Davis Jr.

PRAY TELL

TABLE OF CONTENTS

RENALDO

Sing for me—
In tropes of blue ruin
The telephone is drunk
& I'm afraid to say:
Paulo, there is only this fustian fear
In me now--
Waiting for the clock to tick out all
Our borrowed time

PRAY TELL

Brilliant day for a car crash as it were, to bat dead eyes and push the sky
                                        away from swollen lids
lovely morning noon evening night—
to pant for wet hours in strange rooms bloated on rife wonders, close to love
or some kind of new new murder here on blue knees and blotted back, drained
hours, dismal light, new meat, new anguish, same old taste of blood & bile in
back of the throat now with these needles—needles in my lung, the day tires, sur-
renders again and as the night, this hooded stranger, is here to see me to my door,
I can hear the fiends, the whores there still singing my name down the street, now
down the lane, with wasted words on their used up lips and I tell the hooded face
anywhere away from her—from all of them—I say but nowhere just as near

TRACING VESTIGES

The hopelessness of hope,
the ersatz of the arts,
the malcontents of marriage,
it's all enough to make decent men
throw their first born into the ocean
but luckily enough for myself:
children are but a thought--
I've yet to conceive.

BRING THEM ALL TO ME

You wet gossamer of my purple night
Bring your love to me
Bring me your barn owl dreams
of mice in snares
Bring me your rabid animus
Bring your sharpened knives
Bring me the bones of howling beasts
Brighter than the moon
Bring me your slow whirling tortures
Bring them all to me

IN THE NIGHT IT COMES

In the night it comes
Like a bad sex party
Or an unfixable junkie
To shake up my bones
To clot with my blood
To sing its song of fevers
Like a small brown bird
With a mouthful of dirt
You can't hear it so well
But if you just listen for it
Most nights it is there—
That songbird of fever
Cloaked in my disrepair

THE CRUELTY IS IN THIS

The cruelty is in this—
in the wincing of herons and rain
the cruelty of all in dead-eyed tarts spilt like stuck angels here upon the
ground, the cruelty of love, so sad that it walks away from any who might dare
acquiesce to its torture time & again, these fools giving chase to other fools, so
cruel, the mind is that it would allow such malfeasances, still I know noth-
ing else more veritable, for this dumb head is stuffed with the noxious sparks
of wailing agonies & their inputs, agonies crueler than the death of children,
herons or rain, stranger than time that it should be quite this way

CHURCH GIRLS

Church girls are often kinky
Coffee stimulates the bowels
Death & time are slipshod illusions
Louisiana has a shit-ton of vowels
Everything hurts & none of it is free
The careworn are careless with their hearts
Everyone you go to bed with denies having VD
Clouds are most beautiful just before it's dark
All the white people have our own white guilt
And the blacks, they have the blues
Hate is but the hangman's crutch
And love is just a decorous noose

CONDUIT:

There is no way away from wanting you, I know
There is no solace to rattle down these languid bones

Bovines in the marl-pit
Space snuffs a burnt sienna sluice
Out there in all her entropy—it waits
To carry my albatross home tonight.

POCKET BIRD MINDS

Goaded godheads
Purple moon & then
Surf music too
Men's coats 40% off
Yes, and there is photosynthesis
Foolish folks with pocket bird minds
And the frogs fall off lily pads laughing
@ time-travel & deep-space exploration
Monkeyshines and soft song sings
And at last it comes to take my loves
In a small surrender of flowers & fog

NOW, NOW

now, now

sick with fever
& existential inertia -
their armies of animus
rout the parapets
of my languid mind—
in a pageant
of paltry snarls

now, now

diurnal angst
cum nightly tremors—
shaken here in this place
of death--
I am—the thorn in this lion's paw

now, now

pygmies dance with flames
peony   pray but for rain
kiss kiss same same --
always.... just the same
leeching on to new loves
in the very maw of the thing

now, now

BLUE EVENTIDE

Blue eventide
Soft & shining
Imbues the wan
Spirit of a man
Given to doldrums
With its rousing madness
He who knows the enmity
Of gods & spiders
The dreams of clocks
Still & fabled
He who hears the pulse
Of mountains & tides
The dolor of daisies
Reticent & faint
His own hell now
Like the moribund heart
Of an ill machine:
Cureless & aroused

PAINT HORSES

Paint horses painted all along the walls
Shrill screams and choking children out in the hall
We burned down the house because there was nothing on
To watch as it reduced to ashes in the wet of dawn

BOXER

Necromancy & nihilism on a Sunday
With all the sycophants & sociopaths
Bathos at the foot of my bed
Blood in my bathroom sink
We take it on the chin night in & night out
But we just don't know when to take it lying down
Or more importantly—when to stay there

DEPRESSION POEM

Depression is easy, easy enough for some - for most, in fact. To be despondent over weather, gas prices, or incest, easy enough, right? But depression is more an art form than all of that (if done the right way) you see, depression is its very own coping mechanism: it is an enduring friend who shoves pills and bottles into your mouth. One who will never leave your side till left beside itself for a while so that it may then endure with all the others who come around, to help each of them out when they are in a bind. Depression is there to assuage while you sit in all its godless sorrow. So yes, depression is easy. Easy enough for even myself, as we have our time with one another and then it kindly leaves as it came in but not without a push in the right direction, first. And that part my friend is never so easy.

CRAWL

Sun crawls the sky
Bones crawling
Crawling with ants
Spider in my spoon--
Crawl for me now
Aching drab & dreary
But always crawling
Glass teeth crawling
Saying:
'It's the scarecrow's birthday'
Fogs crawling on needles of grass
Illiterate machine crawling on my sleep
Bland doting of tulips & violets crawl too
Whirring mountain: crawl for me

FAINT HORSES

Freesia bulbs in the snow
Faint horses in the amber
My child of silk sits ill
In her garden of stone
Halfway back to where it was when
We felt it better off to let bleed alone

WHERE WAS I?

I seldom humor the idle talk
of those fabulists and fiends
But I don't suffer fools gladly
Least of all the impudent of these
If not I then you, if not you then I
Not I, so you-
The logician & the shrew

ANOMIE

You tumble to bed

Languid & blue

Torn asunder by

The travails of

Yet another work day

In our contemporary

Consumerist society

You crawl atop the sheets

And lay your head down

In the crook of my arm

Stirring me briefly

Just long enough

To kiss your forehead

And say love you

Good night, darling

Good night

You lay awake—tossing

Back & forth

Fighting off your demons

And absolving my own

Praying with doleful eyes

Both languid & blue

For a death you needn't

Work this hard at

For all the rest of time

For a cold & incessant swoon

When I say to you:

Good night, darling

Good night.

I SHOULD GO

Garnished in an ornate grief—
We cruised the cemetery plot
Where his bones lay bent in unrest
My hand groping your thigh where it stayed there like that
Suspended in stasis
Until you could no longer remember why you should care
Whether it was all over your lissome body
Or otherwise opaque & blue

KANSAS CITY BALLET

When I go--
I hope to remember
the declivity of leaves
from the eucalyptus trees
that arrayed the brick laden streets
of downtown Kansas City
in their gentle ballet of inertia.
Please,
just leave me with that.

THERE NOW IS THE WAY BACK

I see now the spaceman in violet swirls of cream—

There now is the way back. I can see it all—

When I tromp the miracle of snails
When I piss upon the last faint light
When I lift my head up to the rain
When I sing teleology to the herons
When I hack up hydra-headed beasts
When I kiss the feet of lowly saviors
When I breathe disease onto newborns
When I weep my eyes out on widows
When I ponder the behavior of insects
When I humor the cream-puff clods
When I pardon the seasick usurper
When I squeeze eyes out like worms

CAVEAT

I wish it were like this more—
Often, as it were

Axons afire
Sluiced in ignominy
He thinks to say aloud, unlit--

Yes, I've bit my lip even without need
There are actual knots in my stomach

I remember that the Buddha wasn't fat
And erudition is just another word for agony

The syncretic poet postulates
On primordial theocracies
He hews away at Draconian fiats
Gadflies for gods,
Autocratic Demagogues--
Burning the fog away from his glassy pupils
He sits alone in quiet failure
He cannot make good on his promise of making good

Yet he knows that--
From nowhere comes nothing
And no man is that which he's had.

ROMA

In this room I am more relic than these heirlooms of baroque manifestation
More paltry than the sleep of insects. My blood is the blood of ravens.
A sea of sick rain. There are diseased seahorses trawling the Baltic who know my
mailing address but do so very little for my mother's aching. They know how I
could fill ten thousand hopes in my father's empty bottles but instead sate them
with my own despair. Threading needles for the maiden and sending prayers into
fumigated air.
For I have been the tanks of Berlin and the heartache of dejected whores.
I've been the dolor of menageries in factory farms. I have been the hatred of the
hungry. What fucks and bleeds and kills.

FULCRUM

What a striking bit of luck
Just 4 carriages down the line
& she is smiling in my direction
Err—was that a wince? Never mind.
Now we are pulling from the station
This one to my right levels off
A pond of spoor & bile upon the floor
And I take his Adam's apple between
My thumb and the blade closely now
And he squeaks 'eschew, eschew'
But all along the shadowy profile of
This peach vessel: the oaks look deader
Than baskets; the wheat waves out there
All like cinnamon tusks—this one to my right:
An annelid, and straight ahead there
The dead glazed sleeper taking down drink orders
I carp like pubescent pestilence:
"Blood of Christ, love."

INCULT DIGEST

They say fireflies aren't flies at all but rather they are beetles
And dragonflies can't walk even though they have the legs to stand on
They say a snail can sleep for as much as three years without waking
They say the cockroach can live up to nine days without a head

                                                    before it starves to death
They say butterflies taste with their feet
And scorpions can go for a year without eating
I say these flora and fauna are already more intriguing than most humans I tend
to meet

SEACHANGE

When the last lily slithers
From the slattern's fingertips
Death will be an infinite number
And not even elephants will save you
From their spasms of the spirit
Their armies of prepended malaise
God will make known only in the burden
Of every bromidic routine
Friends and family will sit and stand alternately listless
With nothing new to say nor hear
Without hope or even base desire
For the sky has opened out into an empty shuck
And death is the best deal any of us is going to get.

KEEP MY HEART IN A BOX OF SNOW

Staring out the ceiling
At lamplight lovers
And the animals all full up
Of animus now resign their breadth
To the steepened spaces we call
Sleep and in the morning the sun
Will come to scold the freshly bloomed flowers
The man will come to drop the mail off
And to say his pleasantries and no one will think
Much of those animals at all until the night comes
To remind us all yet again how they are out there
Just watching - waiting for us to slip

AN EXISTENTIAL QUANDARY

There are 3 Alzheimer's patients
Sitting in chairs at the nursing home beauty parlor
The nurse walks in and says "Y'all look so beautiful."
The patients all say thank you and look into the mirror
Then one—staring—pauses and says "Which one am I?"

ADELYN

Have you seen my baby?
I don't know where she went missing to
I'm so sorry for everything....
You're in my thoughts
You're in my blood
It hurts like hell, but you're the one I love
She said "why do I keep coming back to you?"

MELANCHOLIA

Melancholia in the waiting room
Feckless amongst the flowers
I'm a bouquet of geraniums
in June
My mouth like gossamers --
Like Sumatran tigers
Like a pair of silver shoes
Eats the snake before the fruit
And my sickly feet like her own
Albescent & poor
Like the melancholia of the moon
Like a deathless pining for ephemeral embodiments—infinitely unfulfilled

MY MAELSTROM SINGS THROUGH FIRE

There is an onus
At the foot of my bed
Mockingbirds mewling
Atop my ceiling fan
And in ephemeral gangways
The gods pass upon us
For we've had our shot
And choked on the loot
Time & again

OF COURSE

There are those who are
Prone to spiral out freely
Of course there are—
Those who can
Lose their minds
Quietly—
In quiet little homes
Perhaps because the stock market
Crashed or their brother has been
Diagnosed with a rare blood disorder
Of course there are—
Those who are studies
In their own meticulous undoing
Of course there are—
Those moved to weep openly
For a busted in can of soup
Of course there are—
Still, no matter the modality they've
Chosen for themselves
The corollary is much the same for all
Those losing their minds quietly
In their quiet little homes

LET US PRAY

Because the tulips have their injury

Because the night moves on itself

Because the neighbors are spies on the dole

Because the bones buried are old as the hills

Because the leeches have no conscience

Because the investment banker dies face-down in her swimming pool

Because the fires lilt from out of apartment windows

Because the mind is itself boundless

Because the body lacks dialectics

Because the lungs expel poison

Because the heart does not discriminate

Let us pray

AGAPE

Honey bees in the tulips
Razor blades in the sweets
The sun sets with seething flame
Whilst you dream of bairns & bouquets
Minuets aflutter through chapel halls
And I hold your face like a broken vow
Something suspended in grief for days
A promise to kiss only each other
The distance from here to displace

CELESTE

Blazing arrays of terse disjoining

Vampires haunt the highway shoulder

Plath with her head on a hot plate

--Snail, leaf, apples fallen from outer space

Moonlight rainbows

Sparkled angel hate

De Sade gets syphilis from a child

Moth eye on speckled egg

Bleeding the artichokes

Butterflies crushed in bestial fist

The words like a caterpillar on your woolen tongue

They crawl out a little more at a time

PALOMA

I lit my friend's hair on fire one time; it was cool.
~ Darius the Convivial.

Blooded arms entangled besides—
Crooks after kisses, sugar for the ride

Flooded temples assume ruin
Doleful hounds perish in the sun
Girls flash their goods for bar denizens
Lorca drags on through the streets of Granada for eternity

Look here, espy the anguish, scan for scars
Stumble upon heaven in a box, dig in for your prize

Bless the relicts, sow the field with salts
Glide like a swan on the surface of comity
Grow your hair out long and brood for a sweet young nestling

Lick your albatross and swoon

STRAY

I took her in
From the cold
Like an animal
And then I took in a stray
Then one day she ran away
And so too did the cat

MAURA
for AnnMarie

If
it's anything
to remember
I remember
your eyes
and their
ageless
sadness

those damn
eyes that
drew me
to love
you when
there was
never
any way
I
         could
                  not

SATURNINE

That stale succor
Clinical in its opulence
Sits at the foot of your bed
Waiting in darkled spaces
For new loves to light out

The open curtain draws in newer agonies—

And I kneel down to weep on your party dress
For things I cannot outrun with whisky or Demerol
Cradling your face, I know how easily I could kill you
But to kiss you would be more daring.

The open curtain waves in wind—
And to love you seemed so much easier before I knew how.

HORSE IN A FIELD

There was this horse in a field
In some old ladies' backyard
I would bypass it every day to work
Every morning I looked to my right
To see if the horse was still there
Roaming free and without barriers
And every time it was just as it had been
It was beautiful and chestnut brown
I smiled every time I saw it out there
Until one day the horse was gone
The lady had sold her home and the horse--
Well, no one knows enough about that to say
But every time I pass that house I still look for it
And I will doubtless look for all my days

HESPERIAN HORSES

There you go, Miss America

Crawling on the ceiling again

One runic wail away this time

And I'm dying to loosen the hitch

Bill says he's been a rebel for so long

That he doesn't know what he's railing against anymore

I'm of the contingency that it's effacement for us both

"Mother's a pale, winsome flower," he posits to me

When discussing our plans for giving up and why it's easier not to

"The great dissuasion in everything," she says

Like an ethical deference for nihilism

Saints with one hand already in the fire

Or "it is what it is" when things get to being hard

WHEN YOU DO

This agony of marigolds is the agony of pinwheels is the agony of cupboards is the agony of miscarriages is the agony of cowboy hats is the agony of wedding bands in garbage disposals is the agony of a woman choking on parsley in Syracuse is the agony of clotted shadows is the agony of children's games is the agony of pay-phone calls is the agony of engines in the night is the agony of turning around is the agony in knowing she won't be there when you do

ROBIN IN MY OPEN WINDOW

Robin in my open window —
Fly—fly away now
Back to your perch
This one's mine.

MARAUDER

Disinclination on the back seat
Craned with sunburned agonies
This: our final clause; a circular flow
Just outside the bathroom stall
Slow horses sleep now in the snow
Vampires bat their eyes at the dawn
Walnut trees bark semiotics to robins
Into the flame, you consume me now
Like sweet poison flush upon my lips
Flippant exchanges in the mouths of arrows
We couldn't have been any more alone

SICKLY SOIREE

This lit out liaison
Now a sickly soirée
It grows gray with stale, sticky flames
Choking the roots of pear trees
& here: your dismal passion—
That timid whore sits slumped
& idle with the hounds of hell
Between that of space & static
In these spastic impasses of immortal saints
Your demons languish at the dawn--its deathless despair
Putrefied perfumes of insect semen squirming
Lips, ton gue, lung & liver
Honey hurts; the shackles shiver
Death wanes—whirls in waves
Bled—we sing to tire out our days
In this dead light painted here
Upon these vacant cellar walls
Like the vines of our fathers' gardens
Come now to crowd their roots

KING SHOT

This anguished antelope light
Eyes drab as water colors
The dead rustled off in twos
Dug out into sand crab sanities
Tear this tide: ebb this lode in lines

This anguish is the notion for eggs & grits at 3am

This anguish of the smoky Big Whig huffing in cigar hells like tar tax stipends

The anguish of assiduous swans tangled in lush tar pits

The sweet pea anguish of products tested upon newborn animals

This anguish of ours: all consuming.

GOSSAMER

I dream in pansies & nymphs
I dream tigers slashing out my sun
I dream the paltry kiss of vamps
I dream of graceless minuets
I dream in street noise & violins
I dream horses on sleeping roads
I dream a death to emulous arts
I dream in faceless pirouettes

FOR THE ONE WHO WALKS IN BEAUTY
LIKE THE NIGHT

My sweet,
Dress the cuts, soothe the sores
That plague my head and feet
Remember:
The grass is not greener on the other side - it's greener where it
eats--
Go—
Go—
Go get your gun, girl!
Your bag of tricks--
Pick a pansy in the rain
Dig your heels into the dirt
As ruinous thoughts assail my sleep
As kingdoms crumble in my mirror
As my killer sneezes in the hallway
Then tell me, what did you see?
How bad could this really hurt?

I MARRIED A COAL MINER'S DAUGHTER IN THE RAIN

Hack the wonder away from my black dreams of laughing clowns
Imparadise me in lies of redolent meadows
Rife with Jacarandas & giraffes
Clock sings its dead math now
Like intemperate old men in prisons of carbon
The giraffe sniffs the Jacaranda
"Nice, isn't it?"

MONA

Episteme & doxa contrast one another
White girls gad in asphodel meadows
Muses take back the art they elicited
Katydids besiege the crocuses--powerless to tamp the first one off
& death betide the surgeon's wife
betimes—
Her hand on the wall, she stings

OBADIAH

That man there:
Face down in a field
of moss;
His eyes, they are
Apricots—
His mouth shucked
& choked with dirt.
Orchids leeching out
from under his galoshes
But I can see not a single
Drop of blood, anywhere
upon his riven body.
Obadiah was his name
or so they said before.

UNTITLED

This hummingbird flits
Like an engine roaring off
The mandrake screams out
When I cull it from the earth
On what is truly
A top-drawer night
To fall in love again
So I will glean my loves
On the hummingbird
The mandrake
The top drawer of night

ROS

dreamt of illuminati
Of beech woods shading paradise
I saw God in ketamine drolleries
And bloodletting on the streets of heaven

I dreamt of Indian headdresses
Of salt on the backs of snails
I saw Nazis crowded amid basements
And vacationers on the Gaza strip

I dreamt of her visage choked in ash
Of flames swelled upon my lover's neck
I saw my father blow his nose with radium
And my mother's bones dance ballet

I dreamt of their anemic armies
Of streetcars cramped in agony
I saw scarecrows whirl about outer-space
And stolen symphonies in languid lament

NOT YET

I've long said
that
in order
for me to find
nirvana
I must first
make my peace
with the rain
pattering on
my head
and this morning
as I stepped out
of my doorway
the raindrops
sang out
to me
and they said:

"Not today, Ole' boy--
no, not just yet."

UNTITLED

So pure a face
For a soul more crass than my own
She leaves me embittered--
Jealous
A disconcerted lover
To take up this cross
The one so built in her name
Carried with shrill cries for days
That rival the auburn locks of hair
Numbered upon her lovely head
And from this cross I shall never be freed
Still whilst I wander I do wonder
Where is she this eve
Are her thoughts extended to me
And in whose bed does she sleep
More fickle than fire
She neglects to make up her mind
With a lover's ache in hand
She bribes & barters
But there's no wager my heart could assign
So now I venture around her
Without dignity's gentle touch
Yet it has never known
My face before

MELINA

Spiders crawl on the clouds
On the flowers—
Flowers of amnesia
Windows of winter
In worlds of TV static
The moon is a miracle
Our aroused brains are tulips
In the anatomy of dreams
Swirling! Swirling!
Tulips & rain
Arrows dancing with madness
Our tongues like squelching engines of dead air
Fascist winter mine
Dance for the dull flame
of my surgical kiss—
Flowers of swirling amnesia
Spiders crawling atop the clouds
Miracles cutting their teeth on the moon

I'M YOUR ASTRONAUT

this poem eats all my cigarettes
drives blind men to fall for the voices
of art school grads & emotionally unavailable baristas
it winks at airheads wearing Garfield t-shirts in the check-out line of the drugstore
this poem is disjunctive without apology
it does not harp on weather, money or poor health
but rejoices in the oneness of all things
its principle is to be kind for no other reason but because it should
this poem feeds on animus & revels in antipathy
its mantra is "people: because life isn't hard enough already"
it tells me love is the devil & that heaven is his greatest lie
it writes to strangers, says, I need you just to hear me when I tell you I'm frightened
& I don't entirely know why
this poem hangs down its head, tries its hardest just not to cry

www.ingramcontent.com/pod-product-compliance
Lightning Source LLC
LaVergne TN
LVHW091232080426
835509LV00009B/1254